Who Are You When no One is Watching?
An Adult Coloring Book for the Loner Inside You

Flower the Dog

PUBLISHED BY:
Flower the Dog
Copyright © 2018

All rights reserved.
No part of this publication may be copied, reproduced in any format, by any means, electronic or otherwise, without prior consent from the copyright owner and publisher of this book.

Disclaimer.
The information contained in this ebook is for general information purposes only. The information is provided by the authors and while we endeavor to keep the information up to date and correct, we make no representations or warranties of any kind, express or implied, about the completeness, accuracy, reliability, suitability or availability with respect to the ebook or the information, products, services, or related graphics contained in the ebook for any purpose. Any reliance you place on such information is therefore strictly at your own risk.

No Skin No Preconception

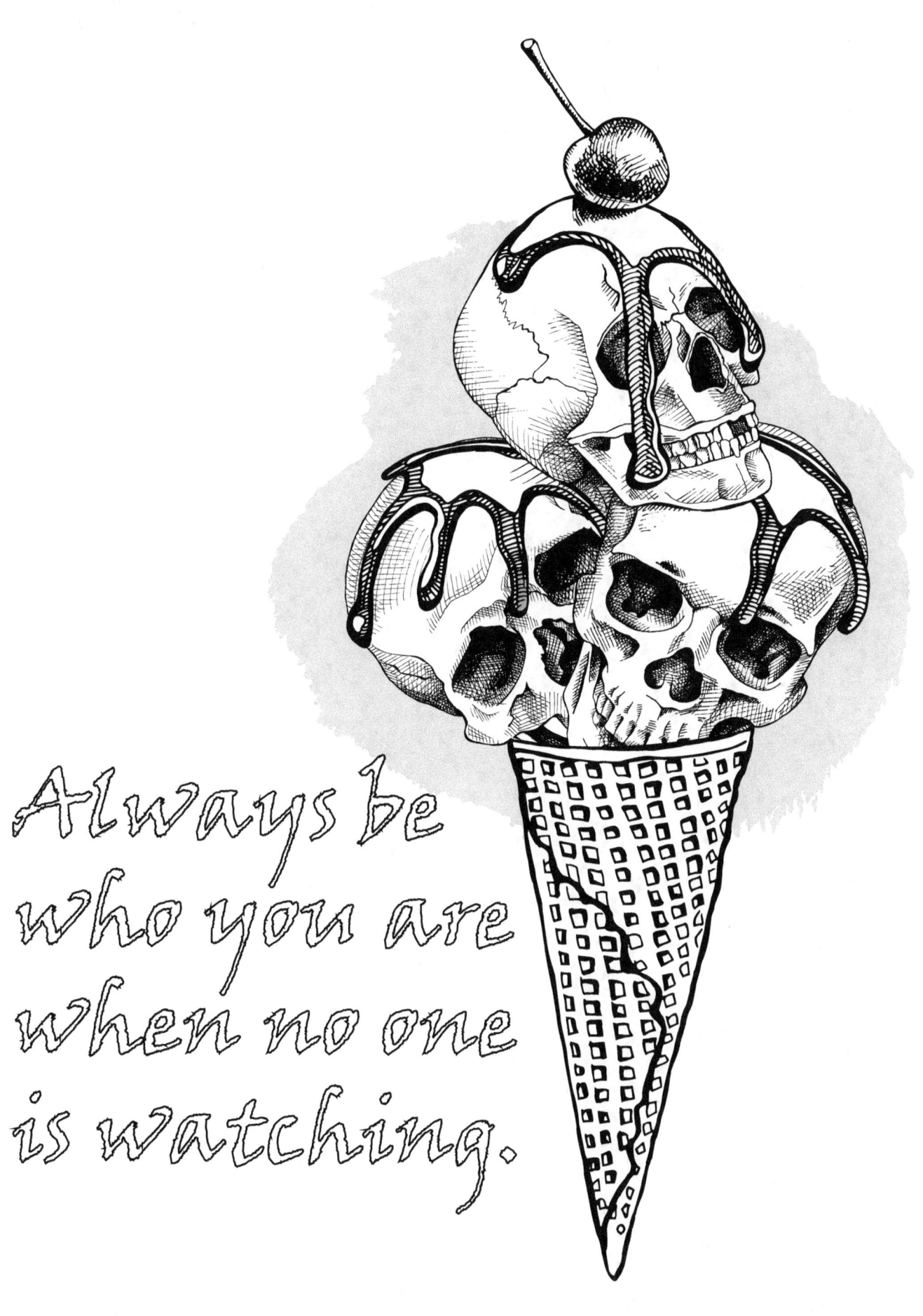

What color is your soul?

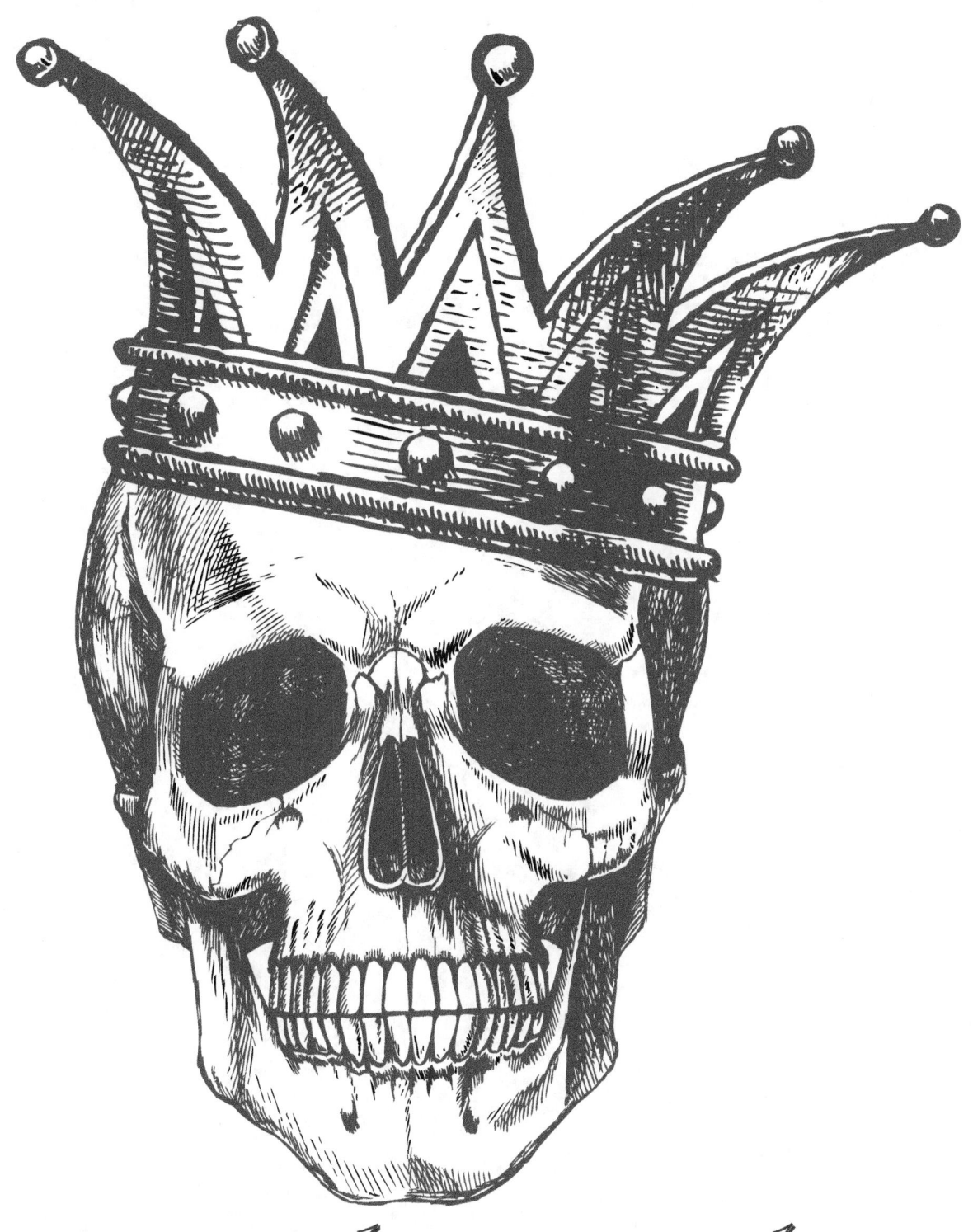

SURROUND YOURSELF WITH PEOPLE WHO USE EMOTIONS TO DESCRIBE YOU.

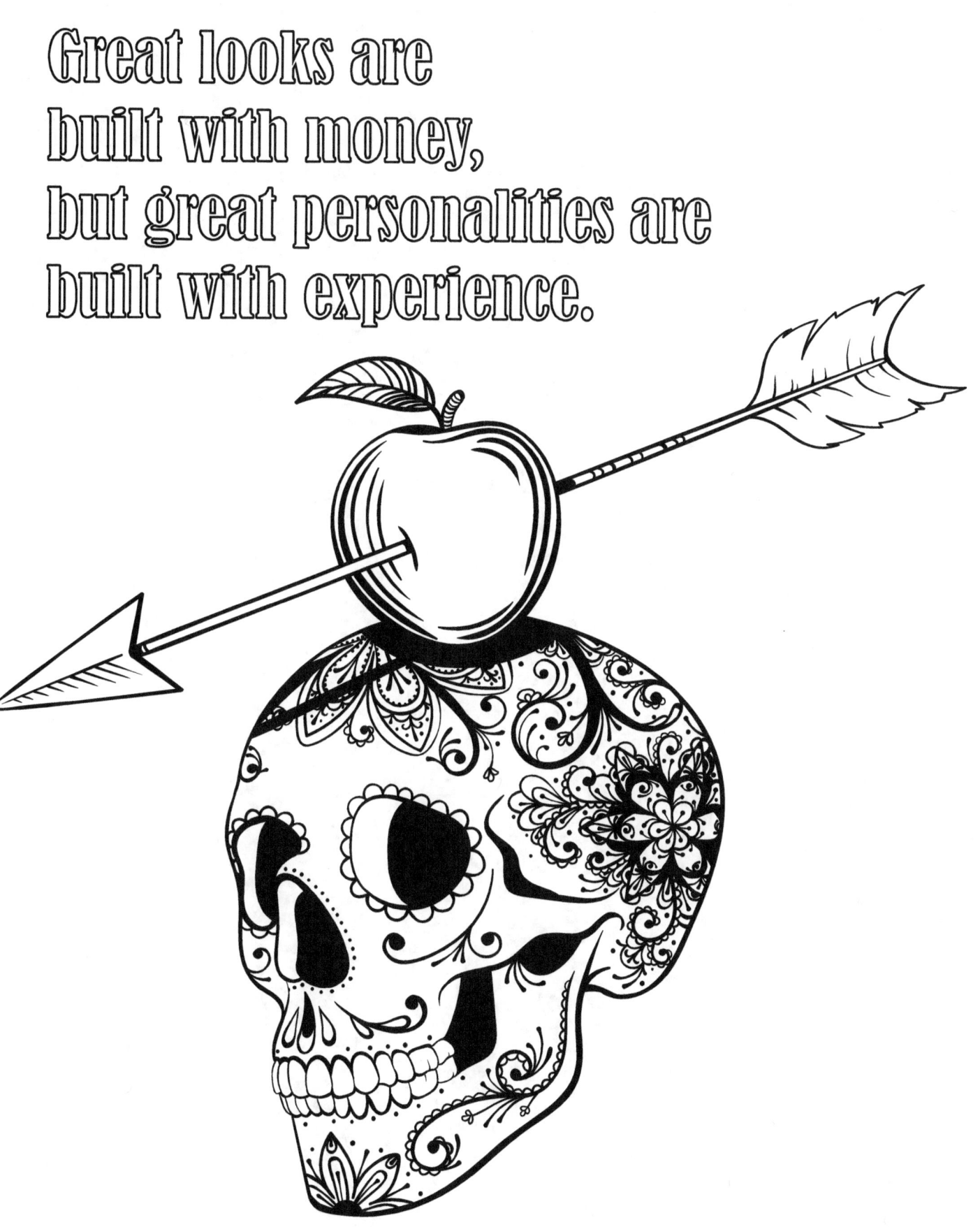

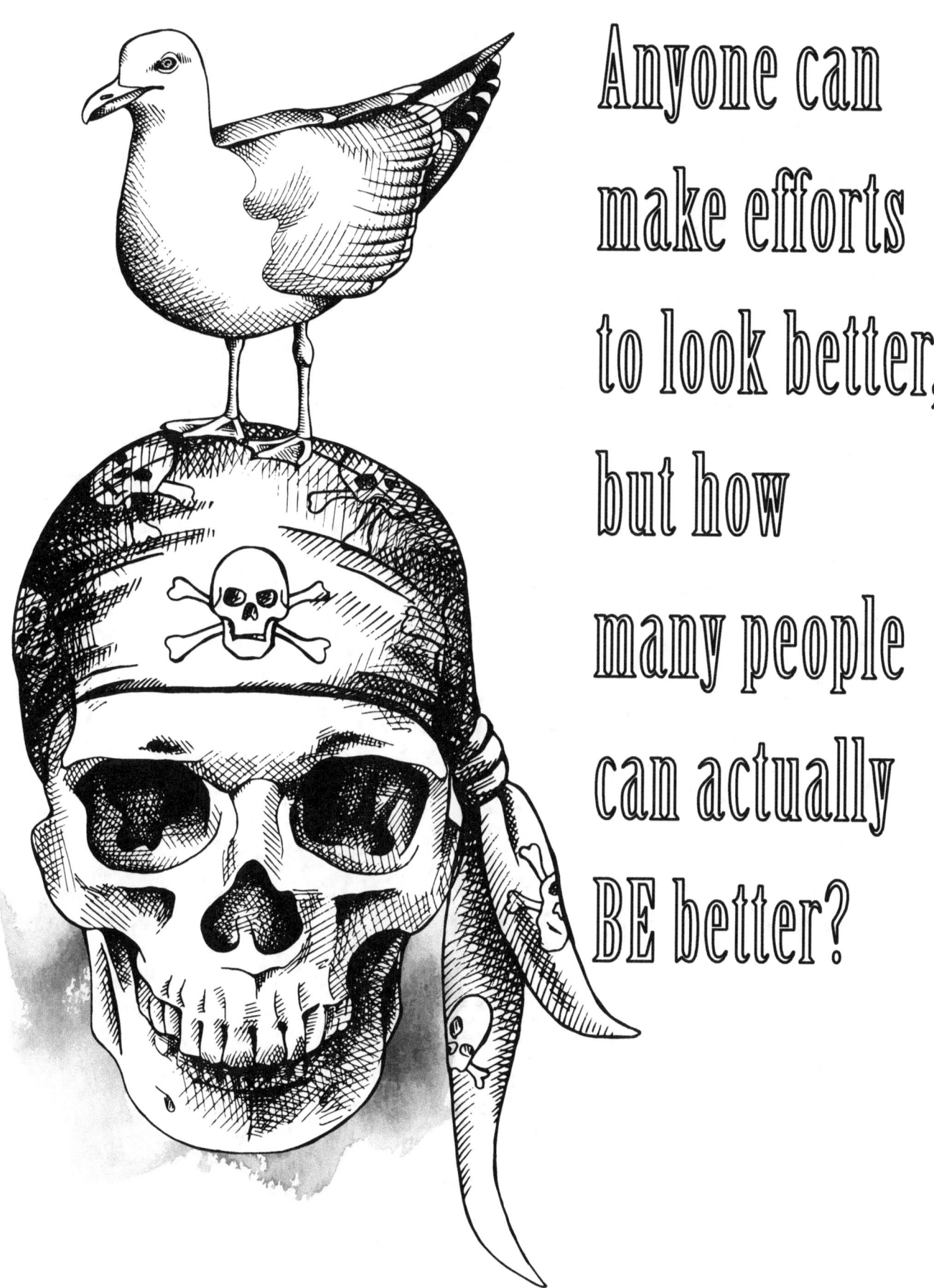

The greatest qualities of human beings come from the inside.

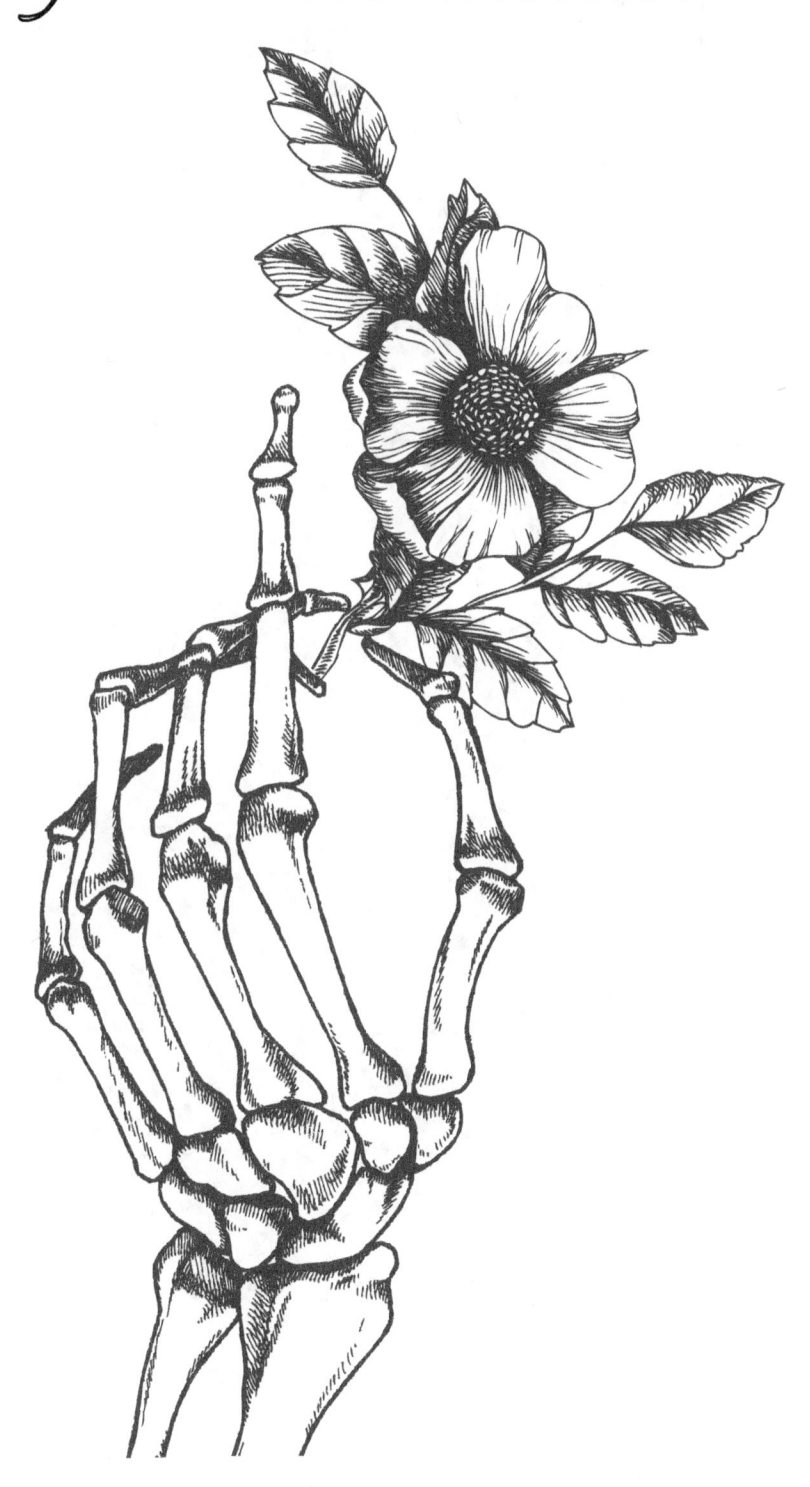

The world's greatest people are remembered for their passion, their drive & their achievements.

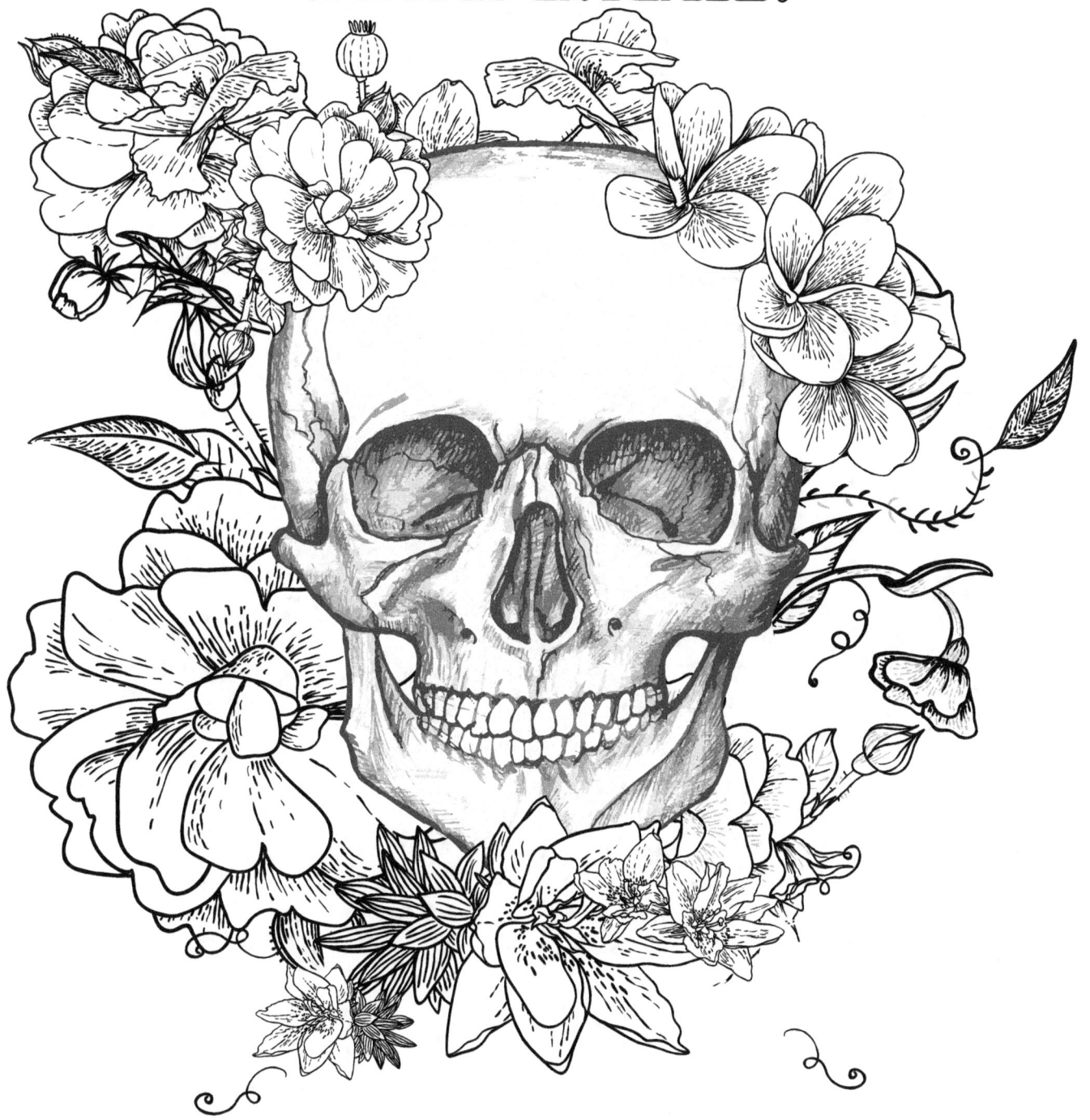

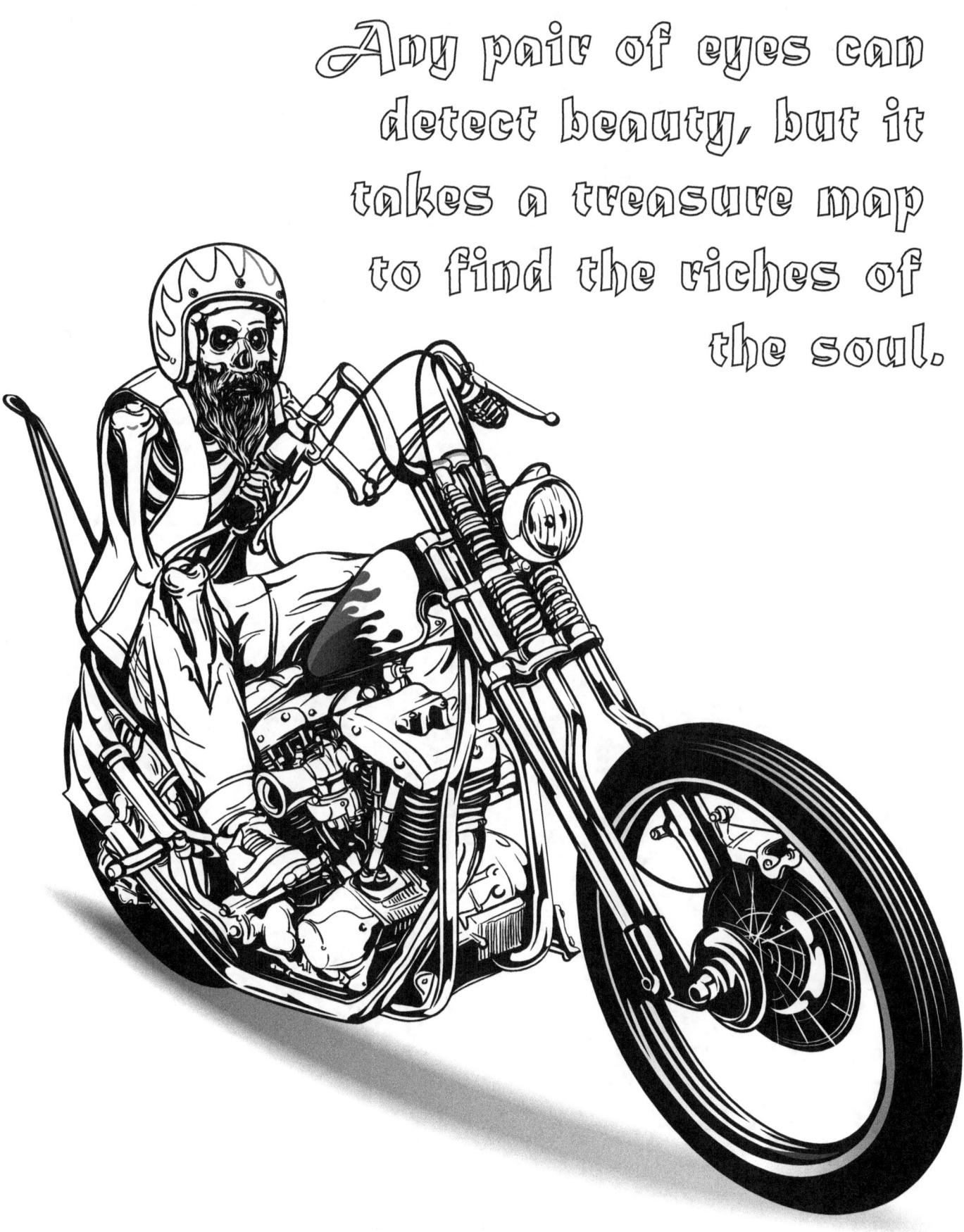

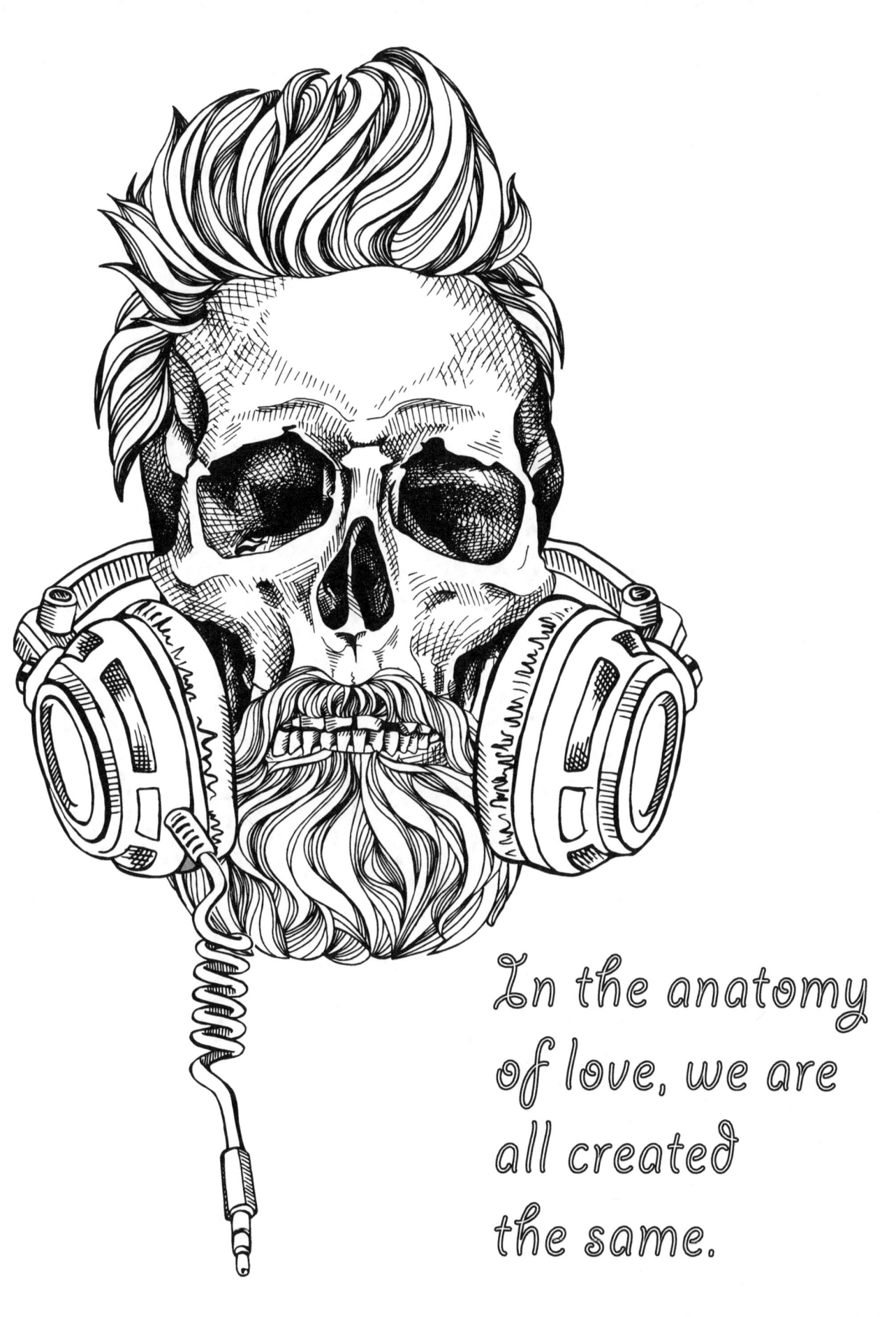

If you had to choose between external & internal beauty, remember: the latter never ages.

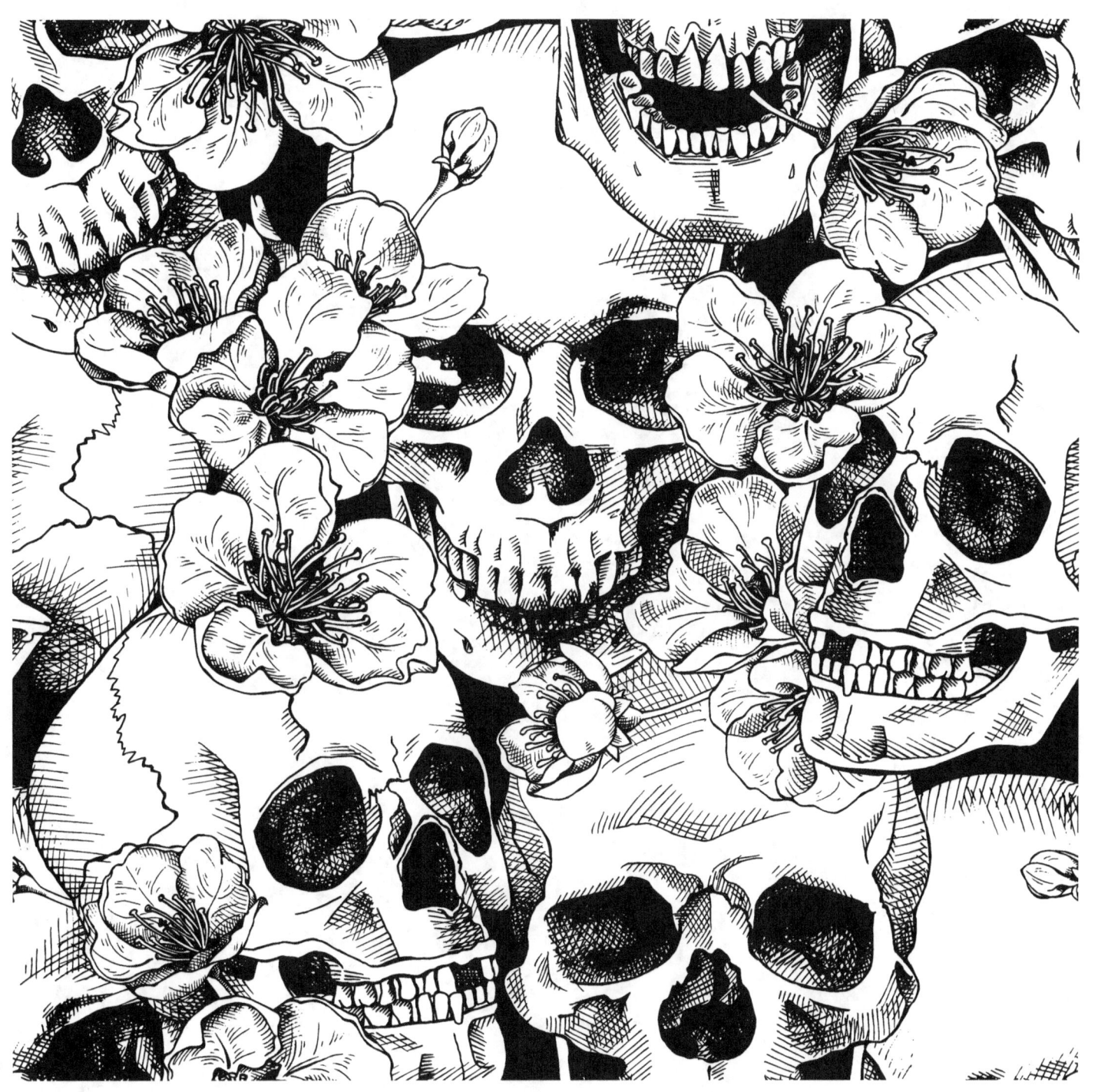

It takes one day to get a complete make-over. It takes a lifetime to change an ugly soul.

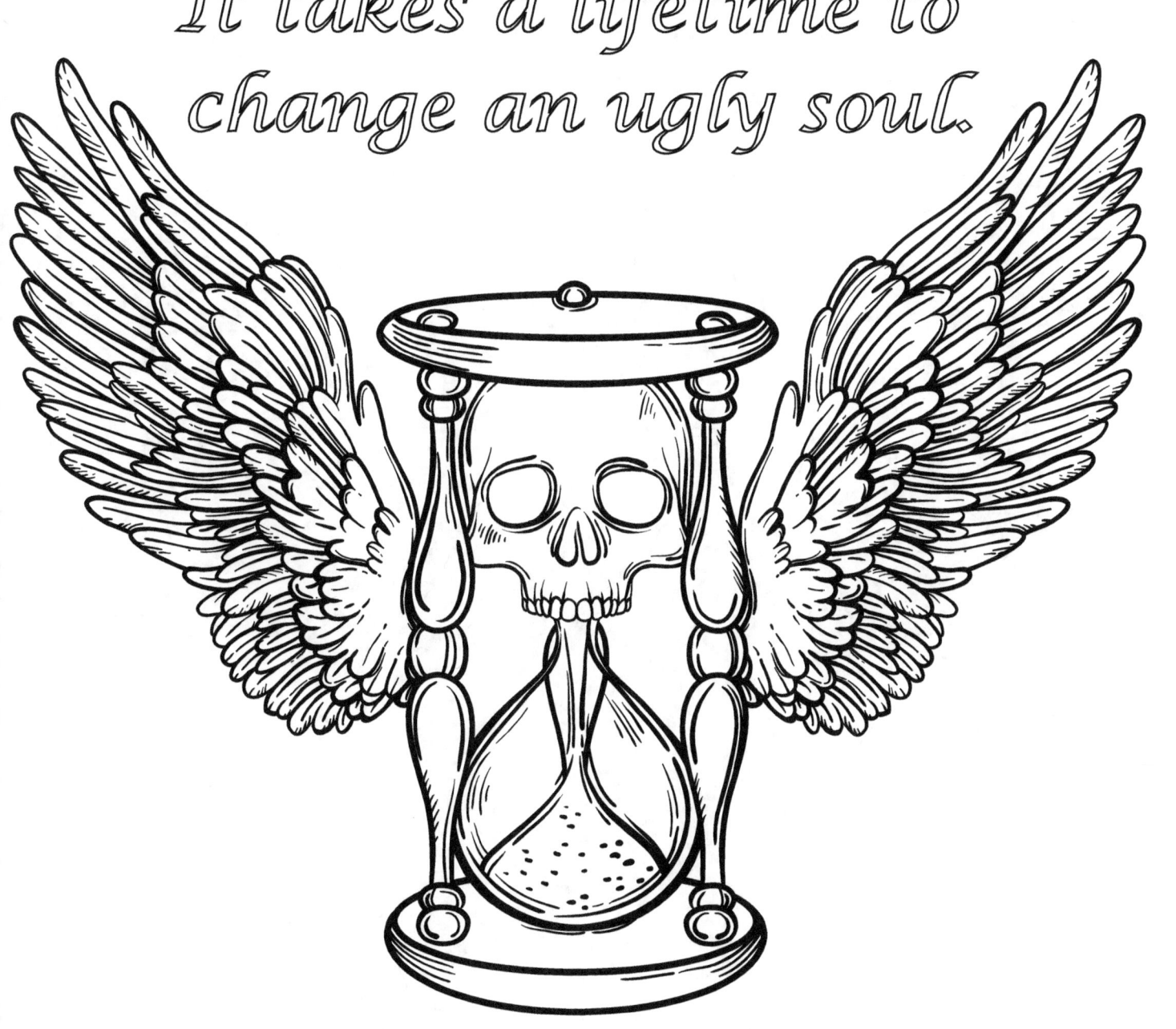

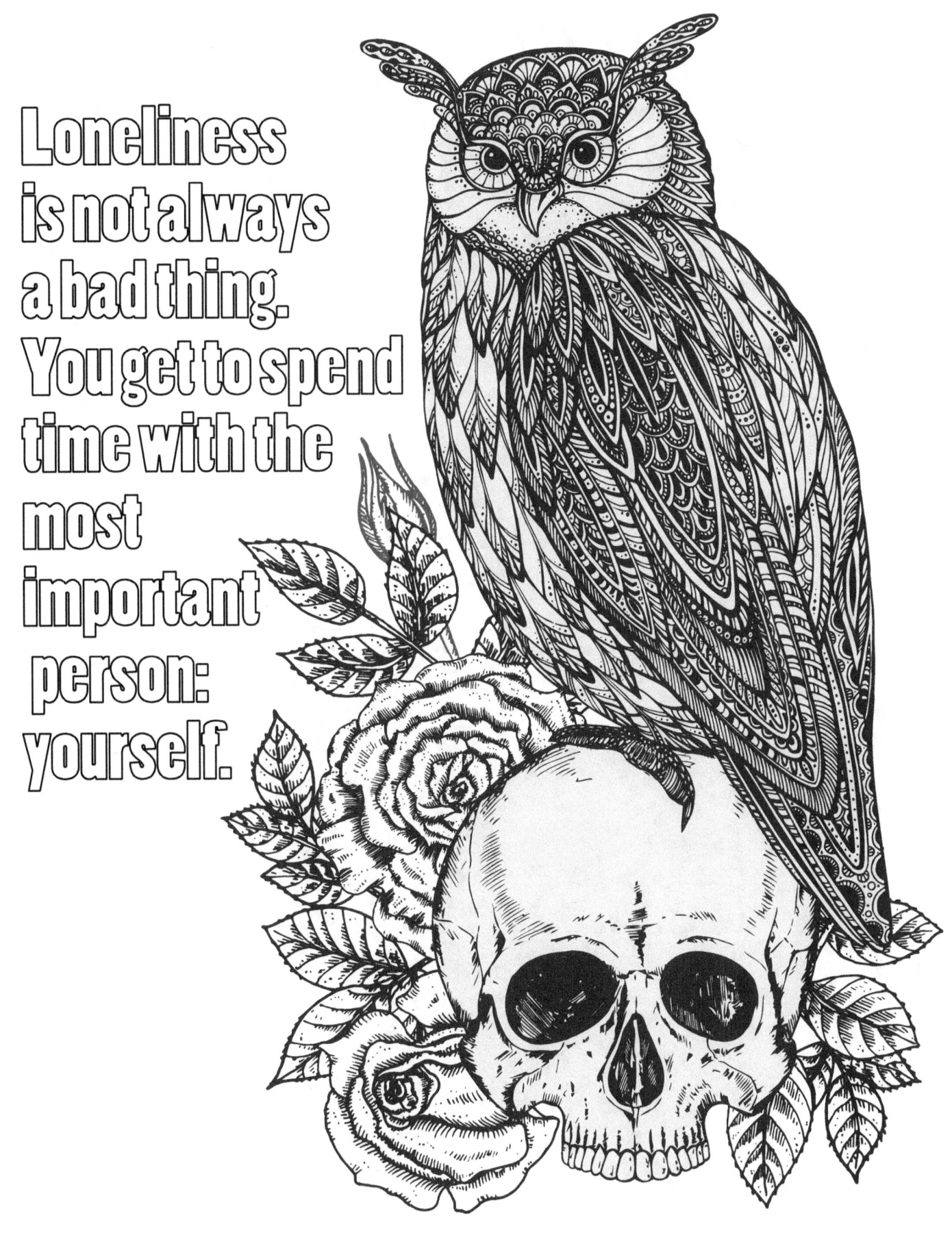

Loneliness is not always a bad thing. You get to spend time with the most important person: yourself.

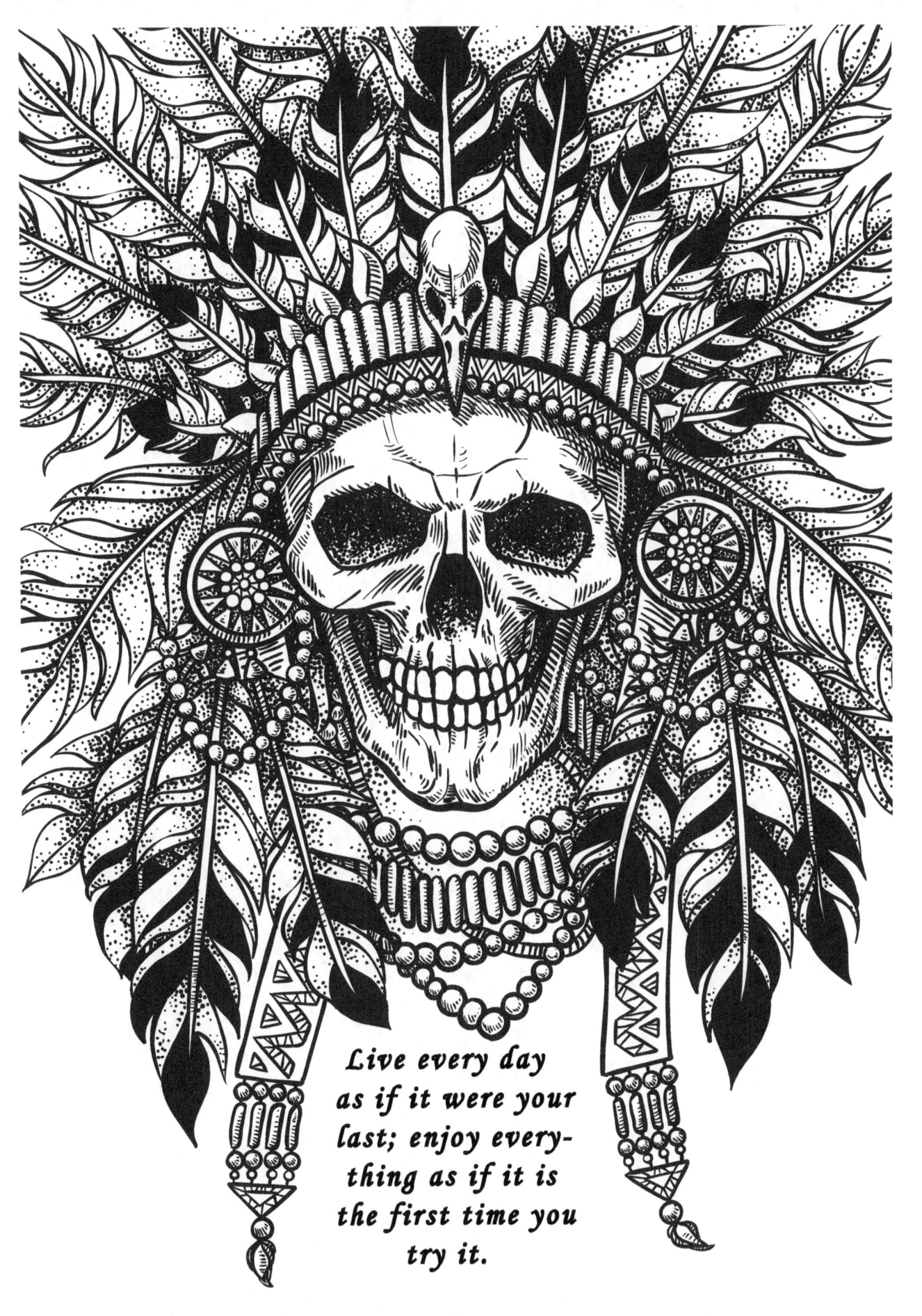

Only by having been in the dark do we learn how to appreciate the light.

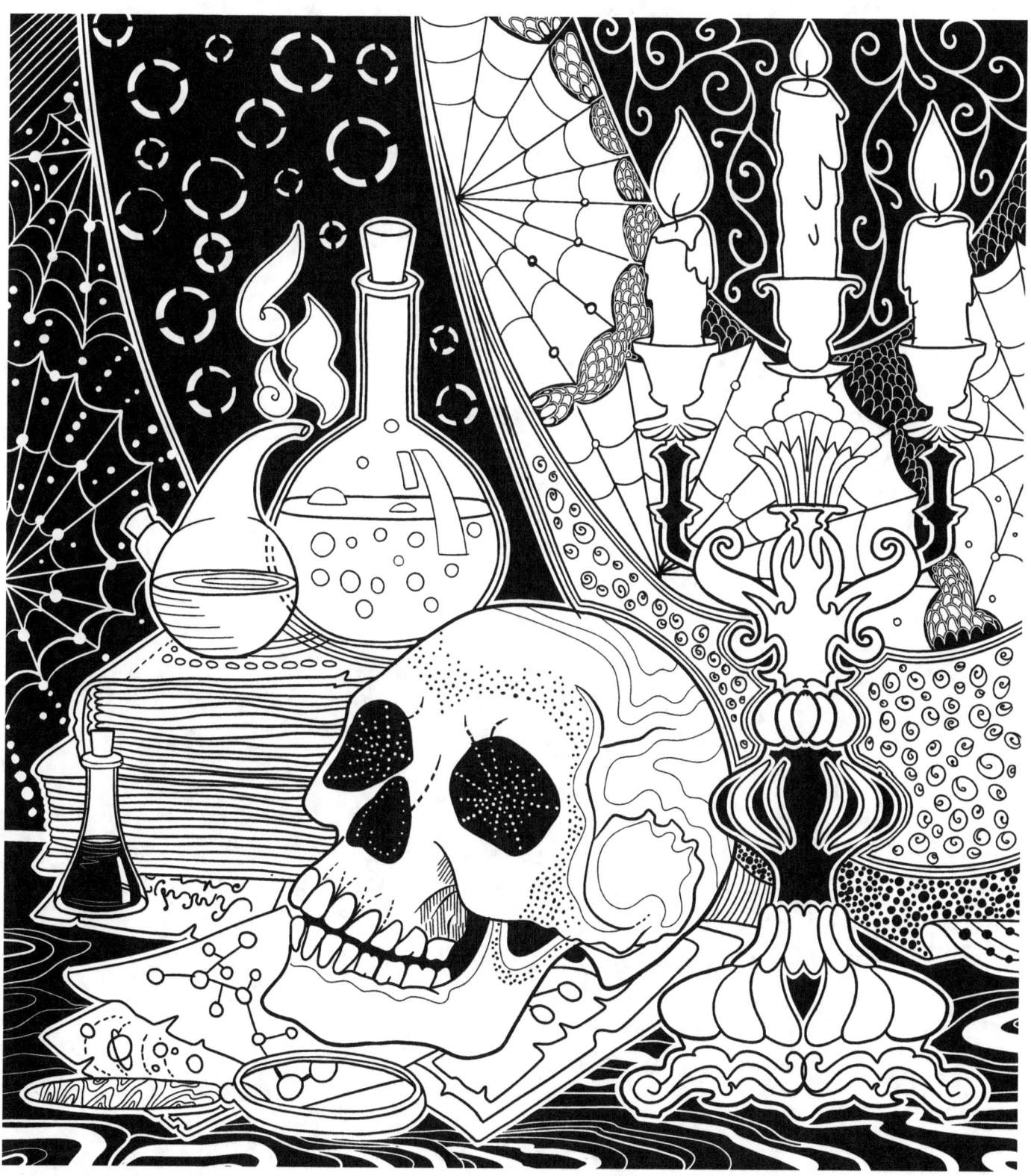

Being selfish is not always a flaw: it's how we survive.

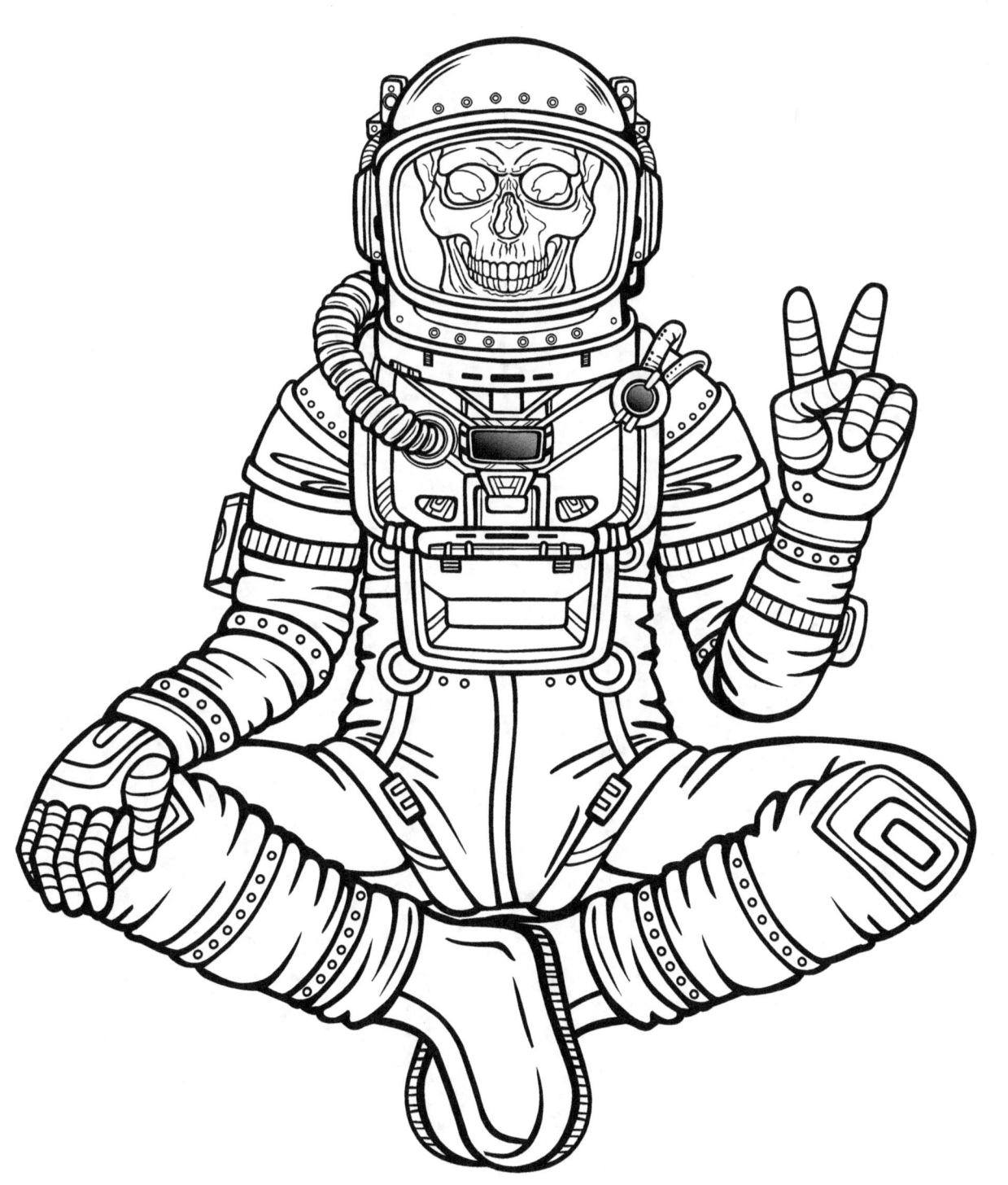

Learning to love yourself is one of the hardest things you'll ever have to do.

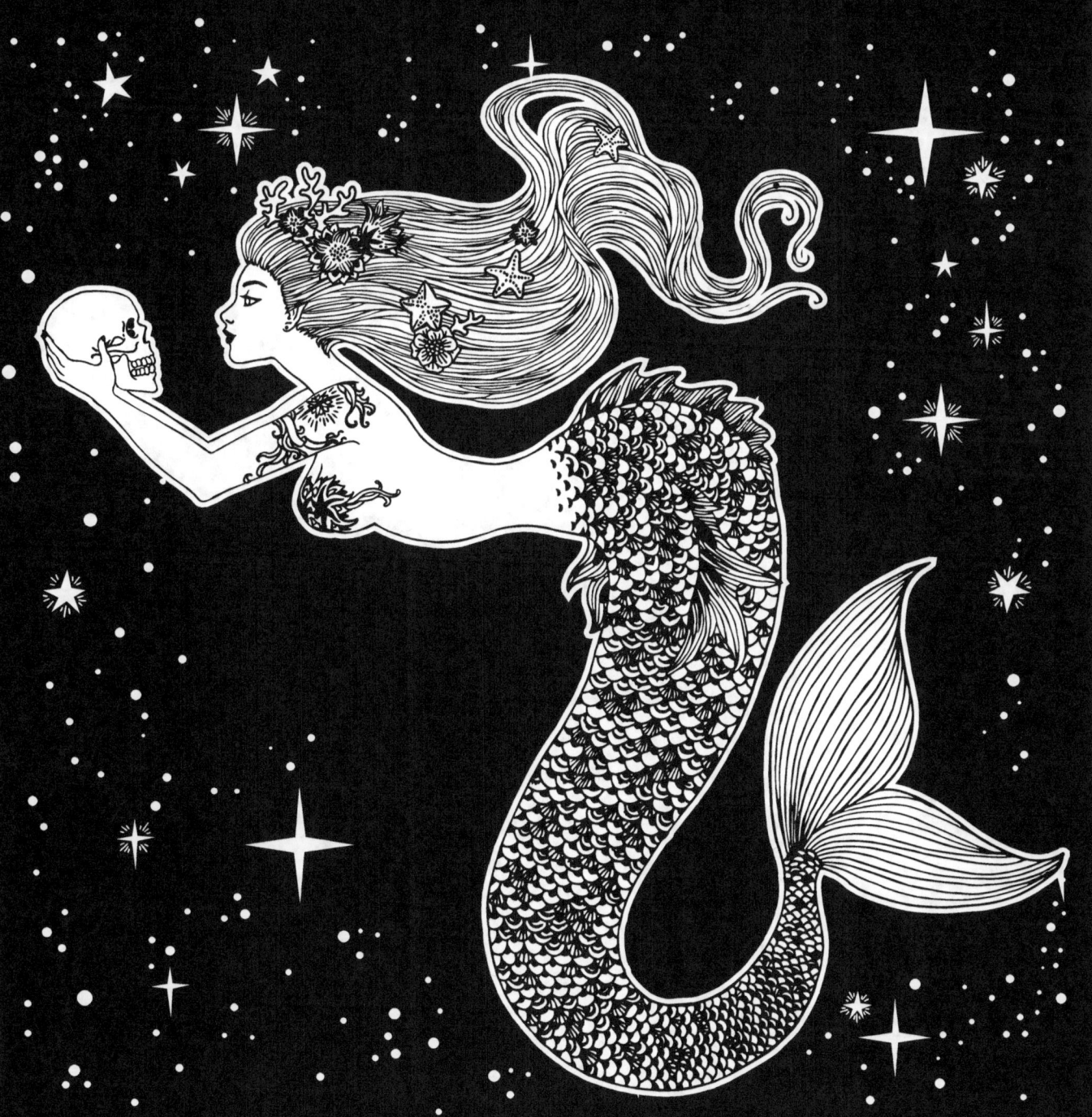

Always fight for what you believe in.

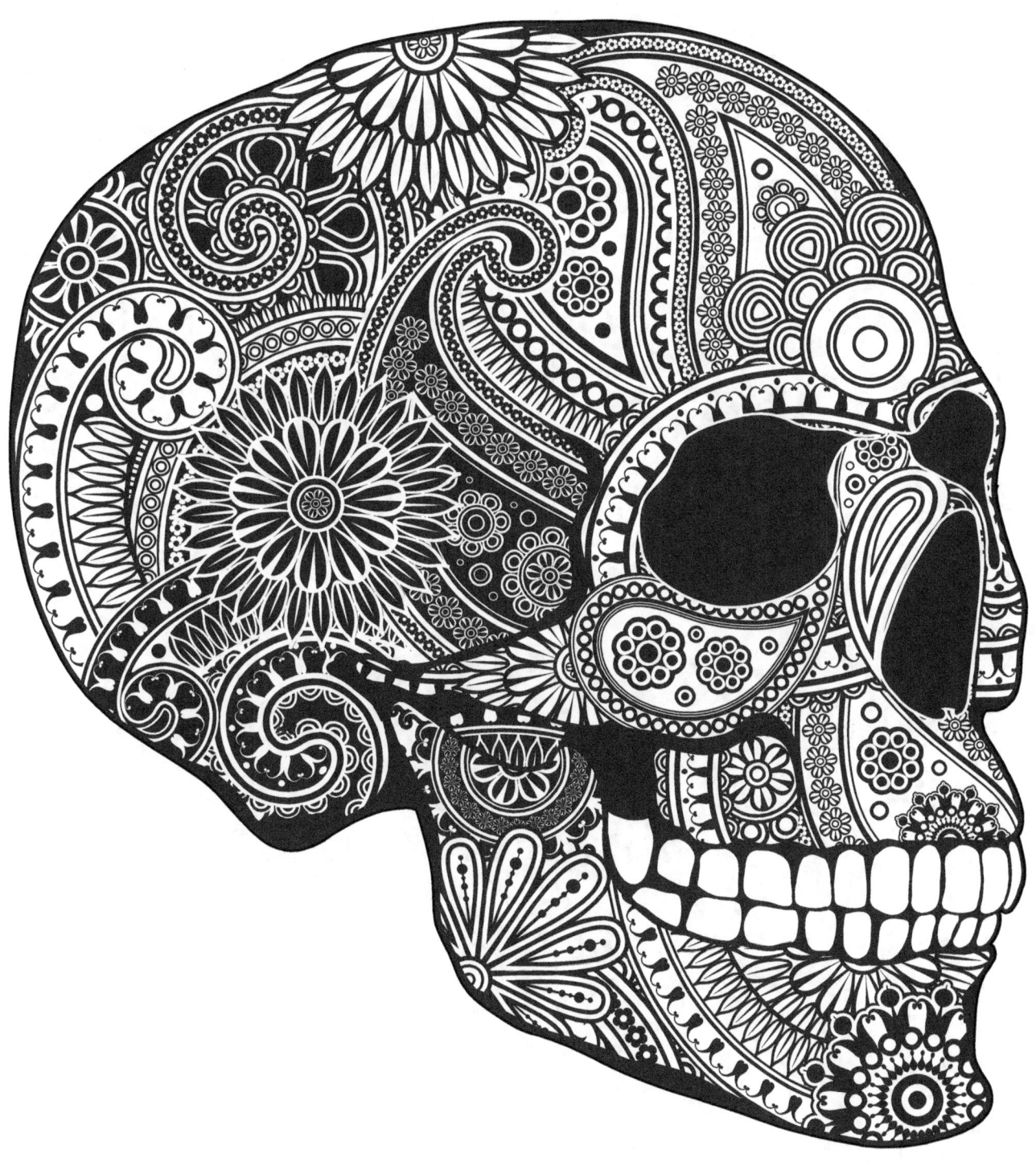

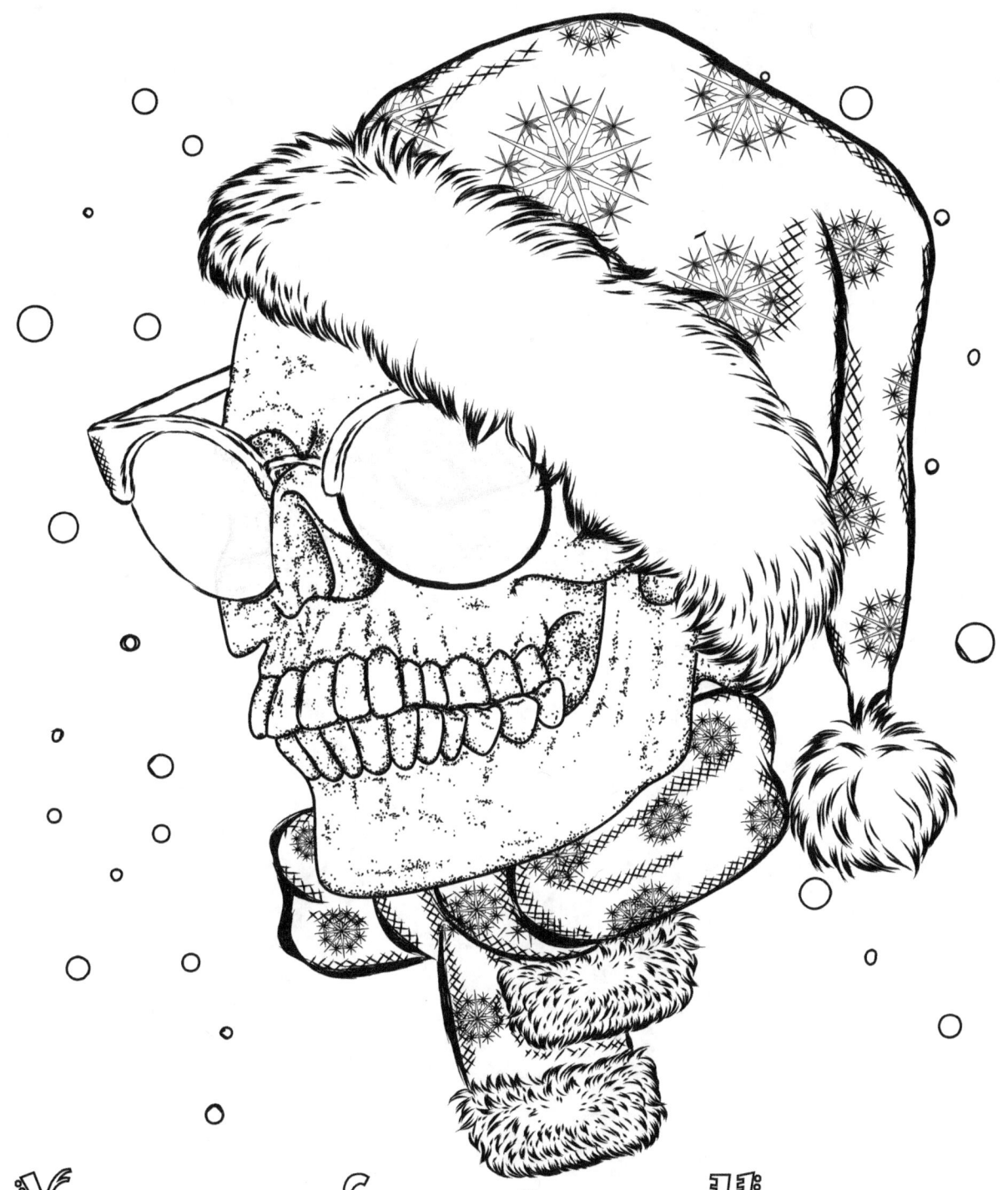

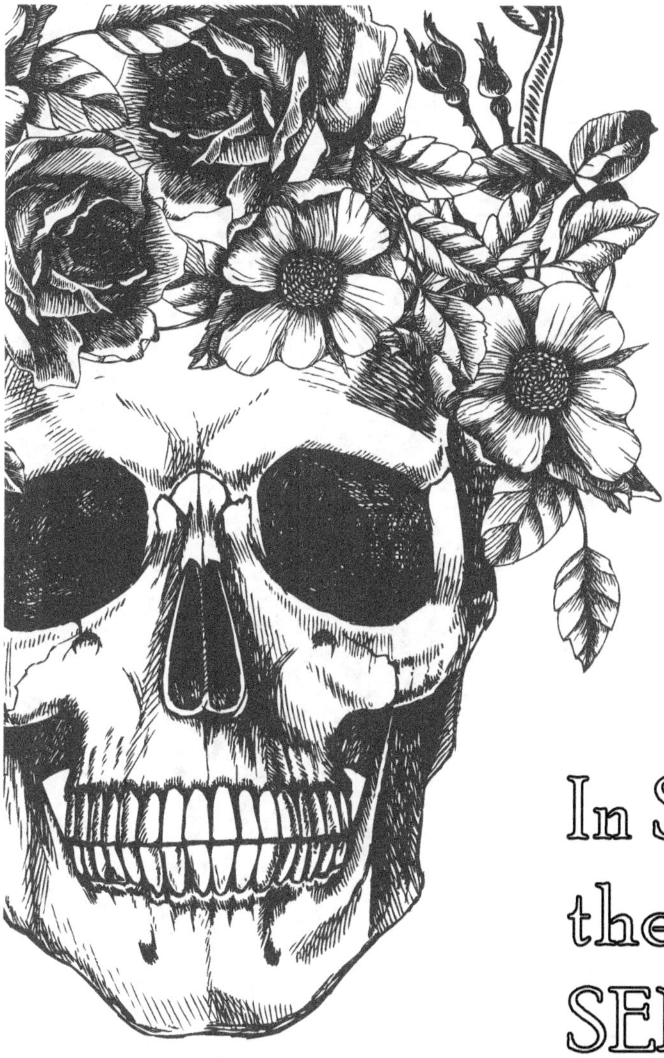

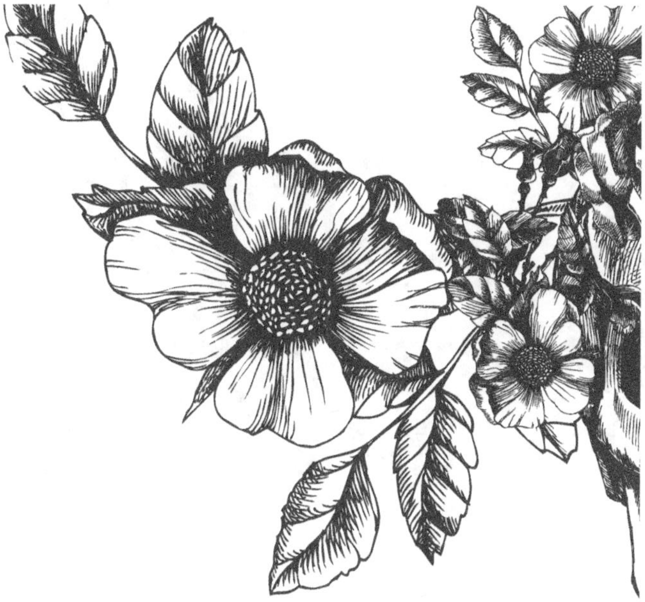

In SUCCESS,
there is no room for
SELF DOUBT.

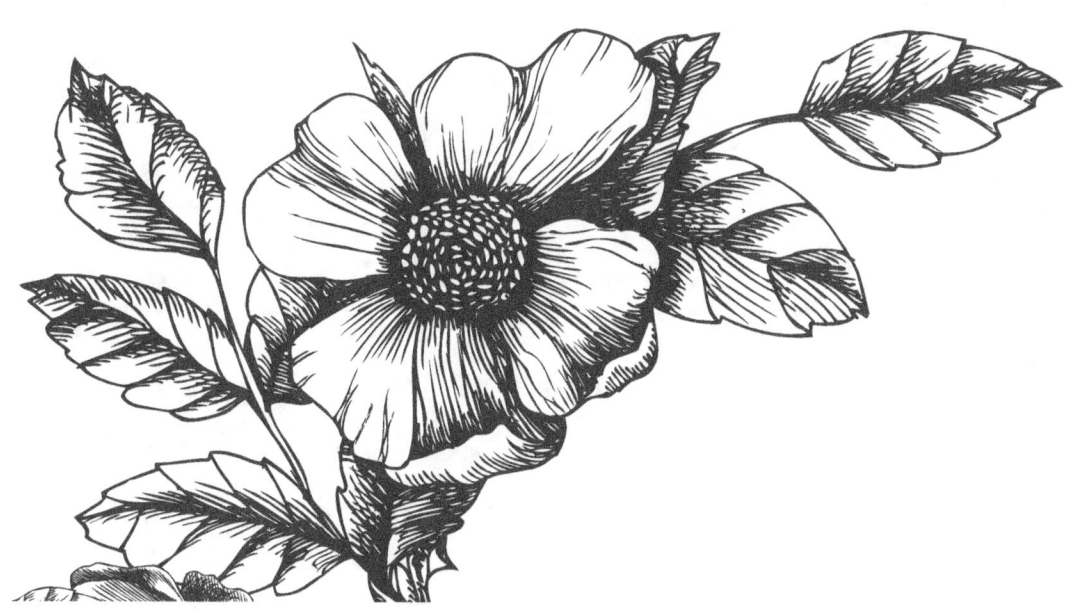

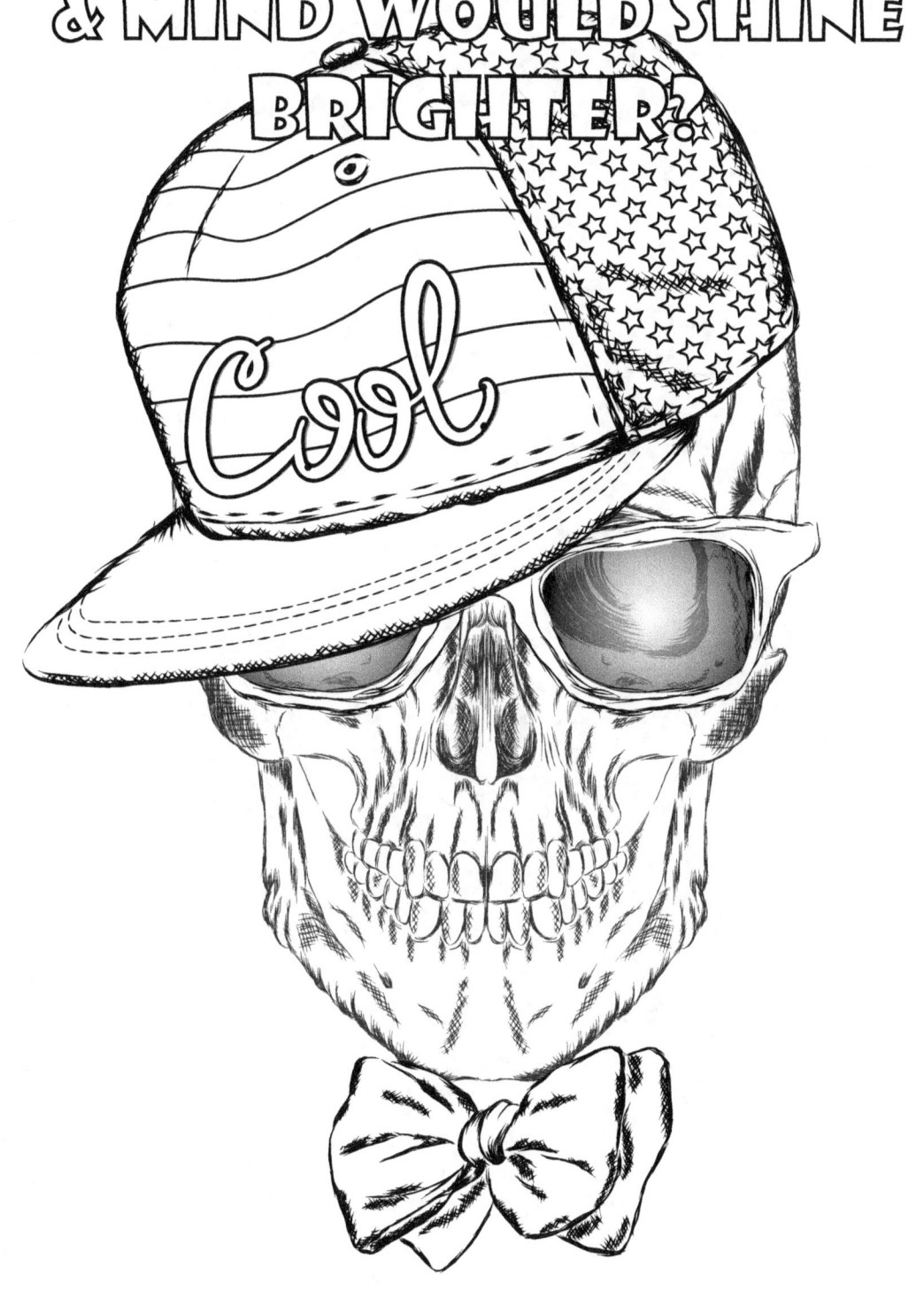

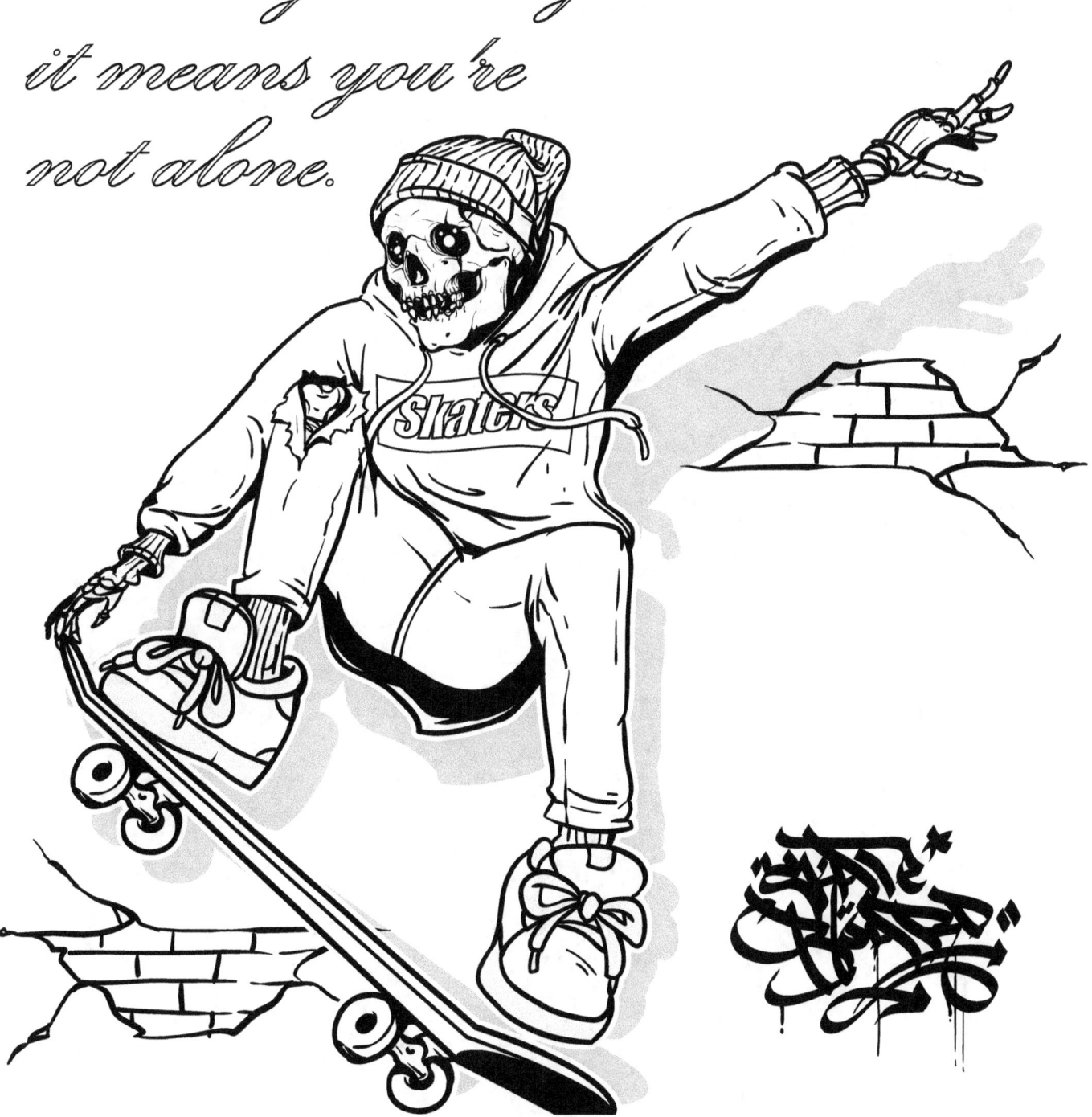

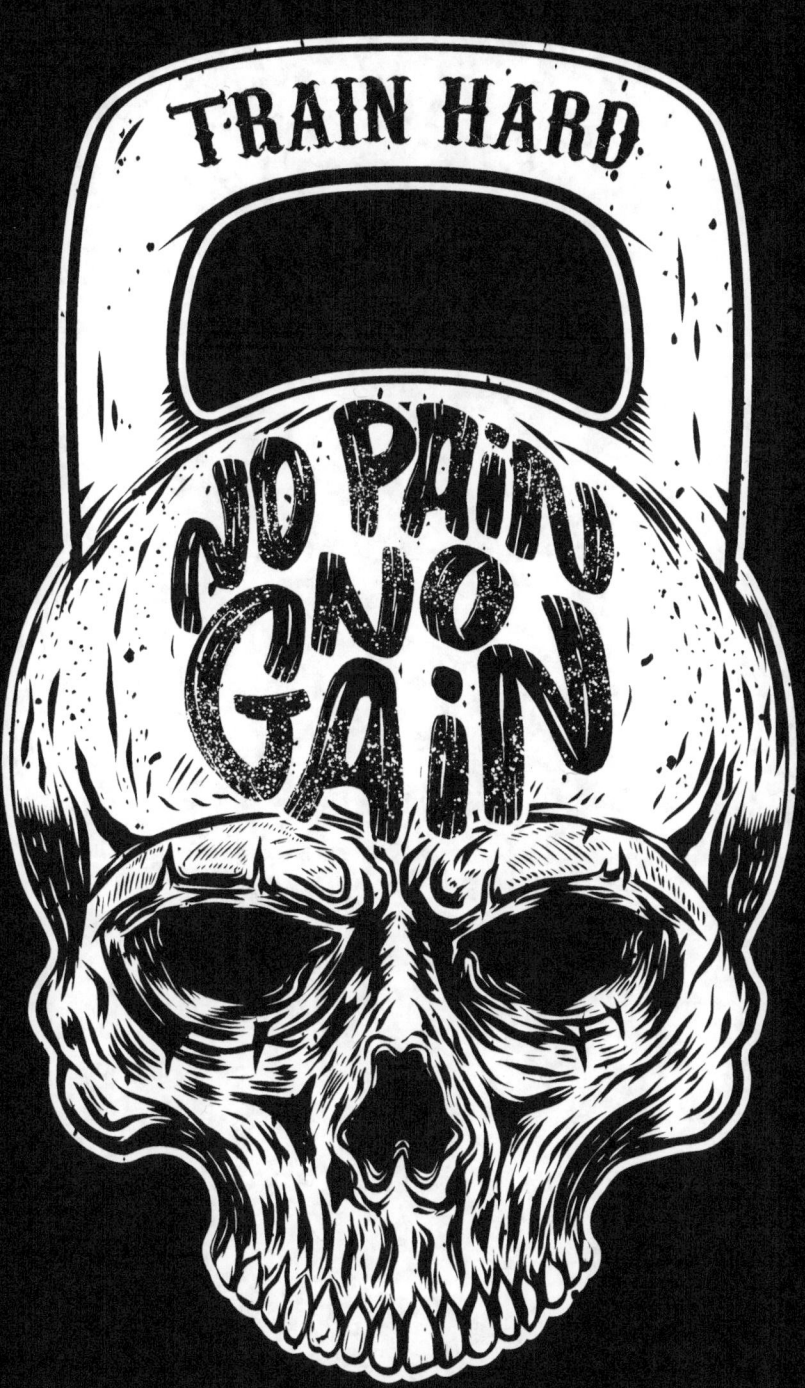

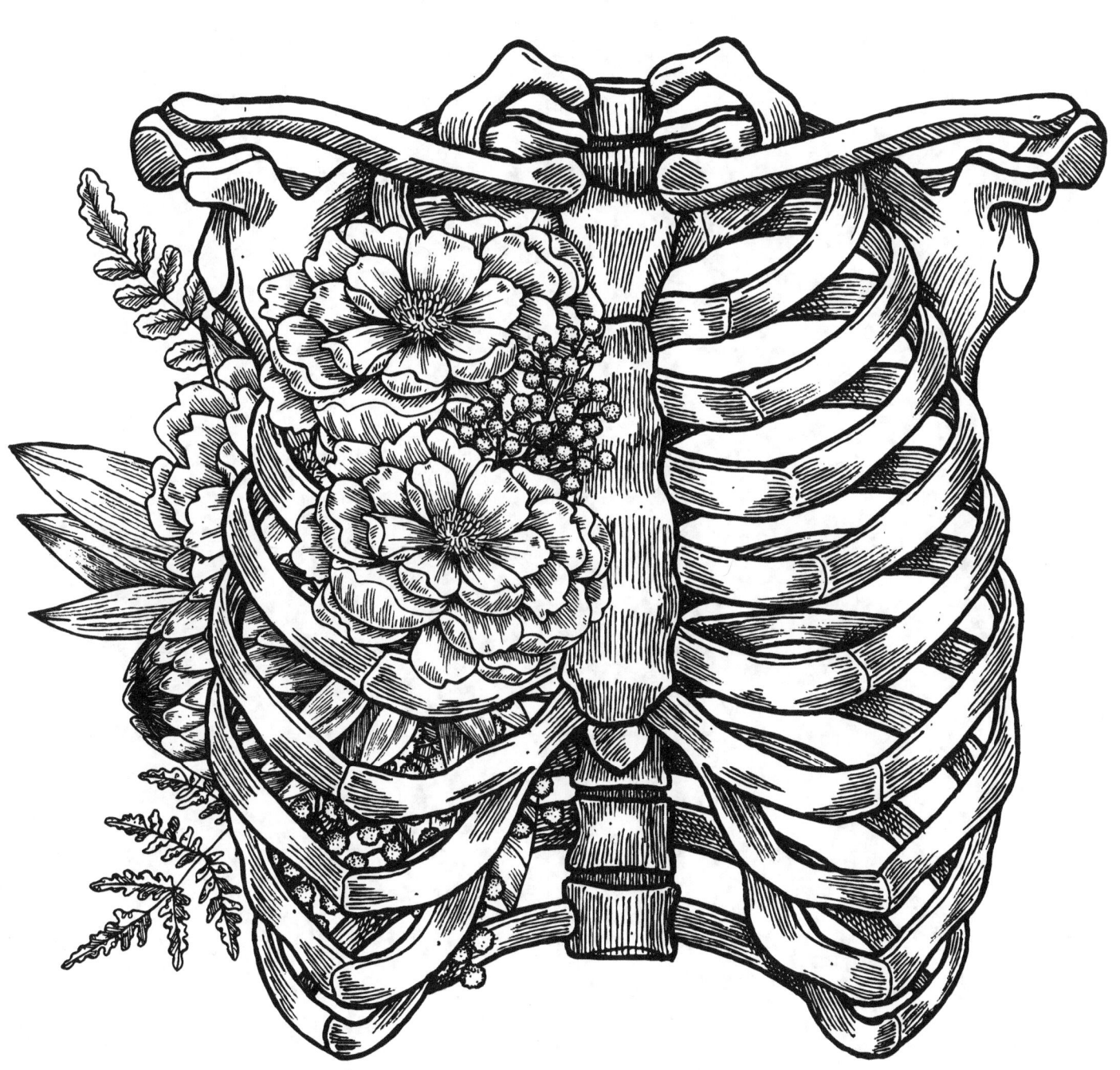

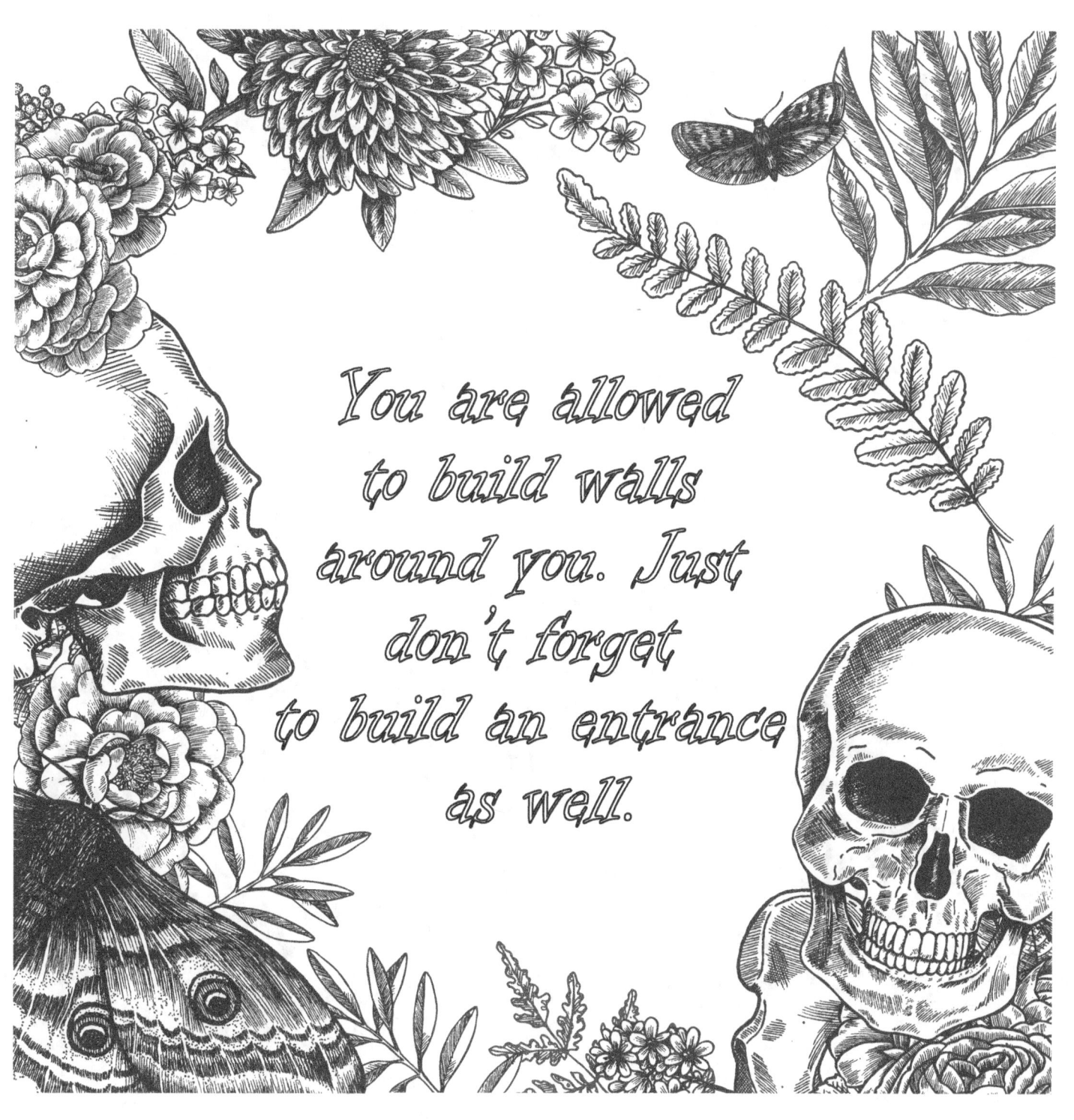

Every negative experience in life is worth it, as long as you learn something new about yourself.

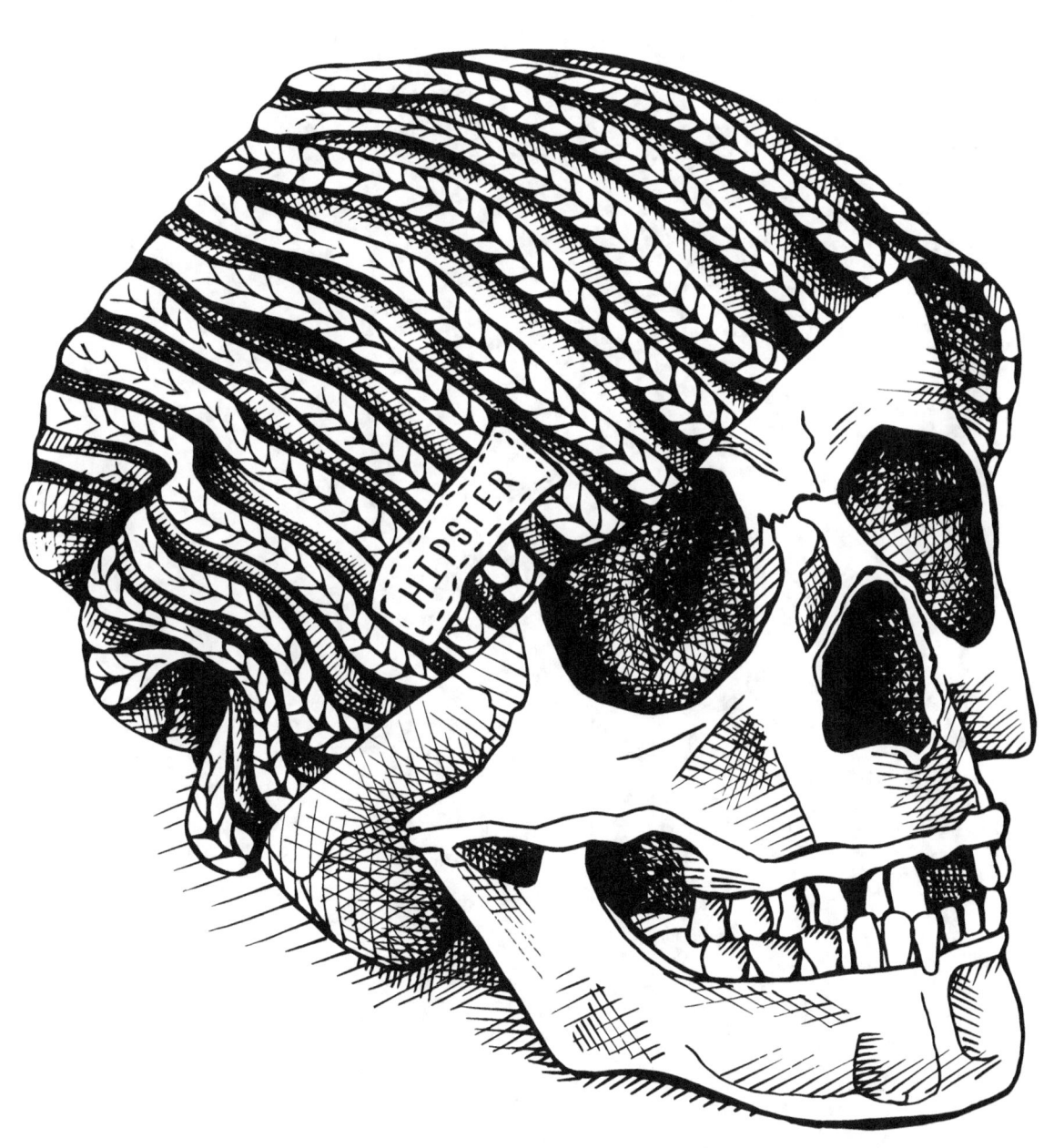

The moment you finish building self-confidence, nothing in the world can ever bring you down.

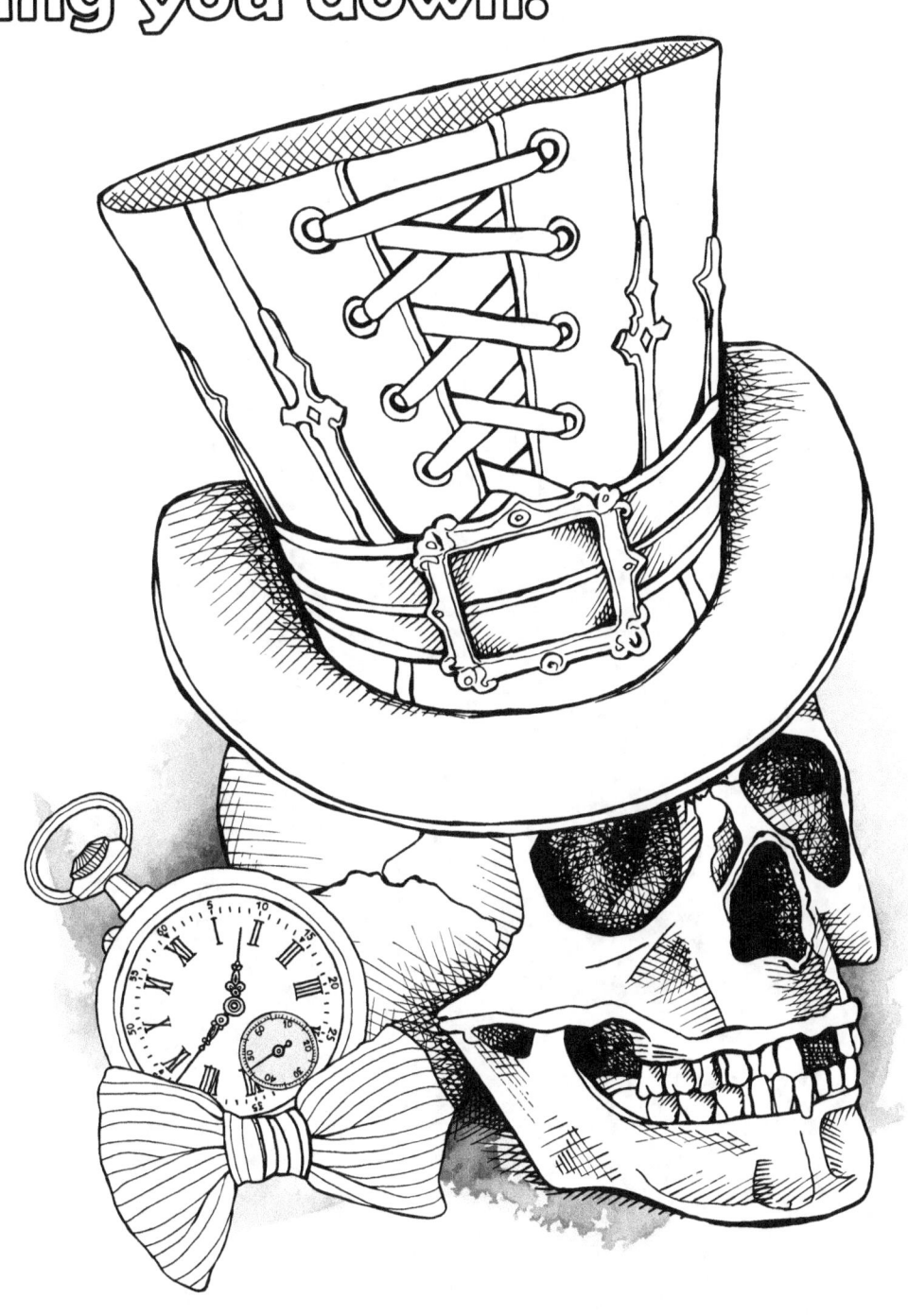

ALWAYS BE THE KIND OF PERSON YOU'D

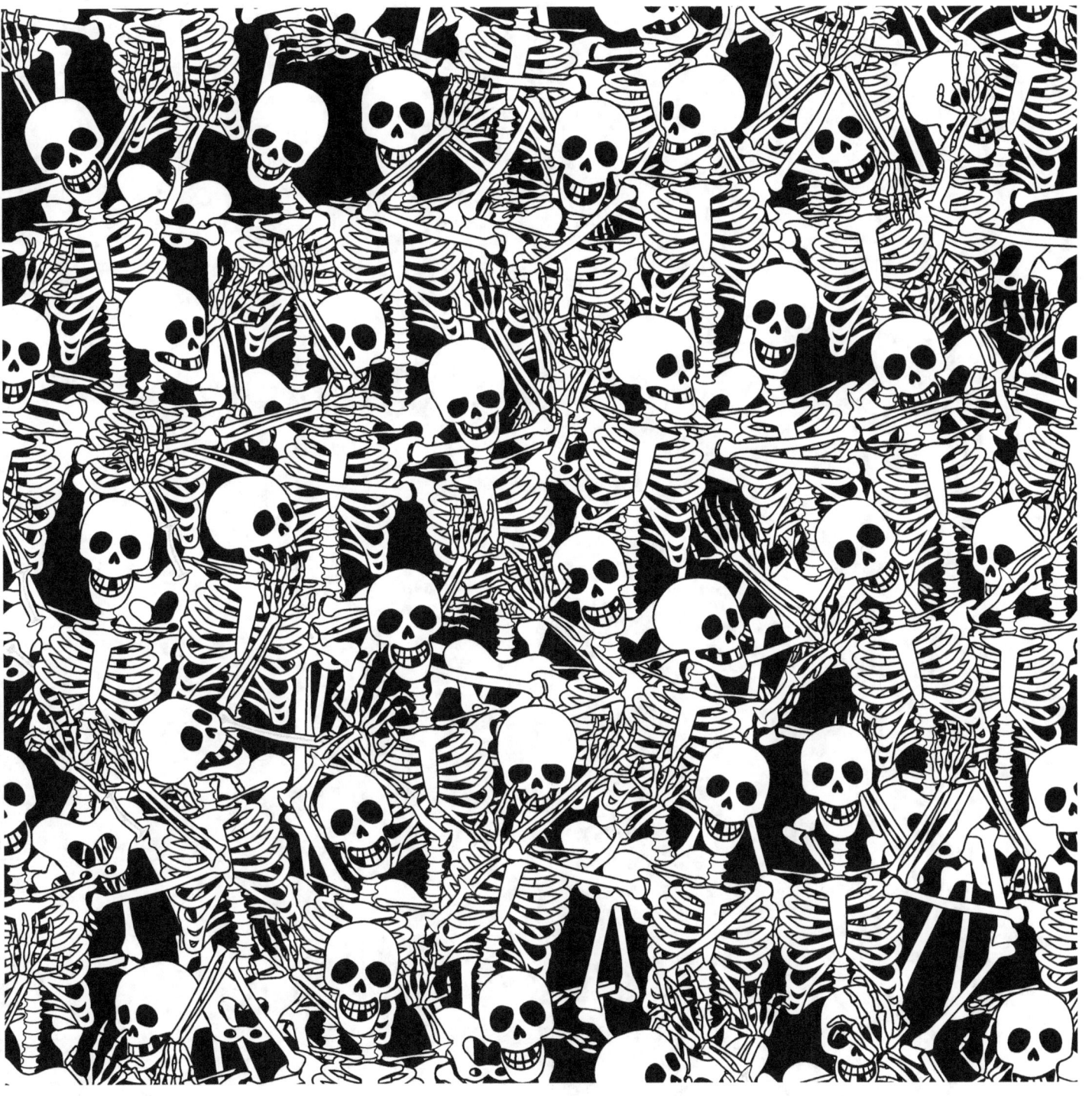

WANT TO SPEND YOUR ENTIRE LIFETIME WITH.

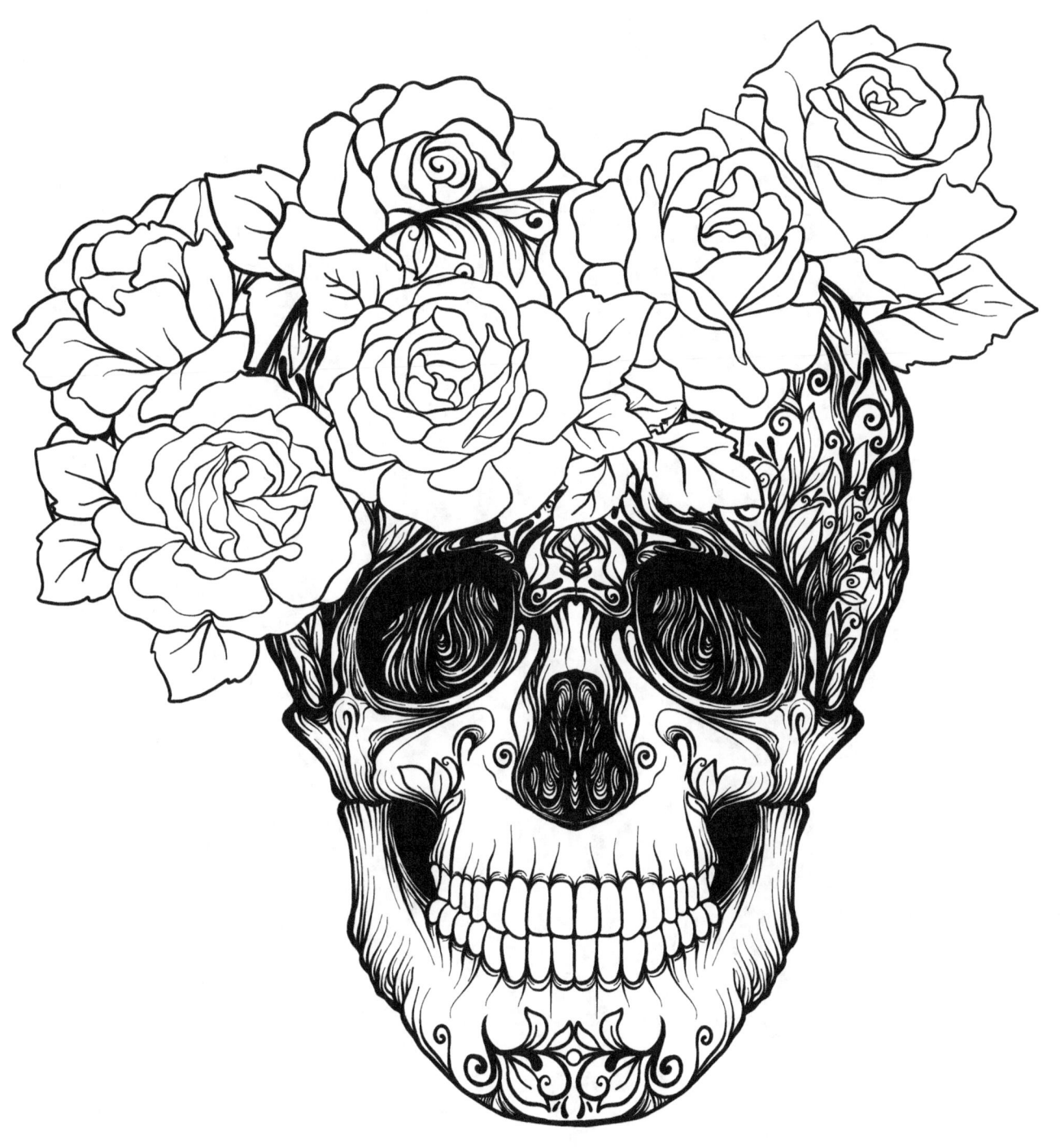

It's called humanKIND, not humanBEAUTY.

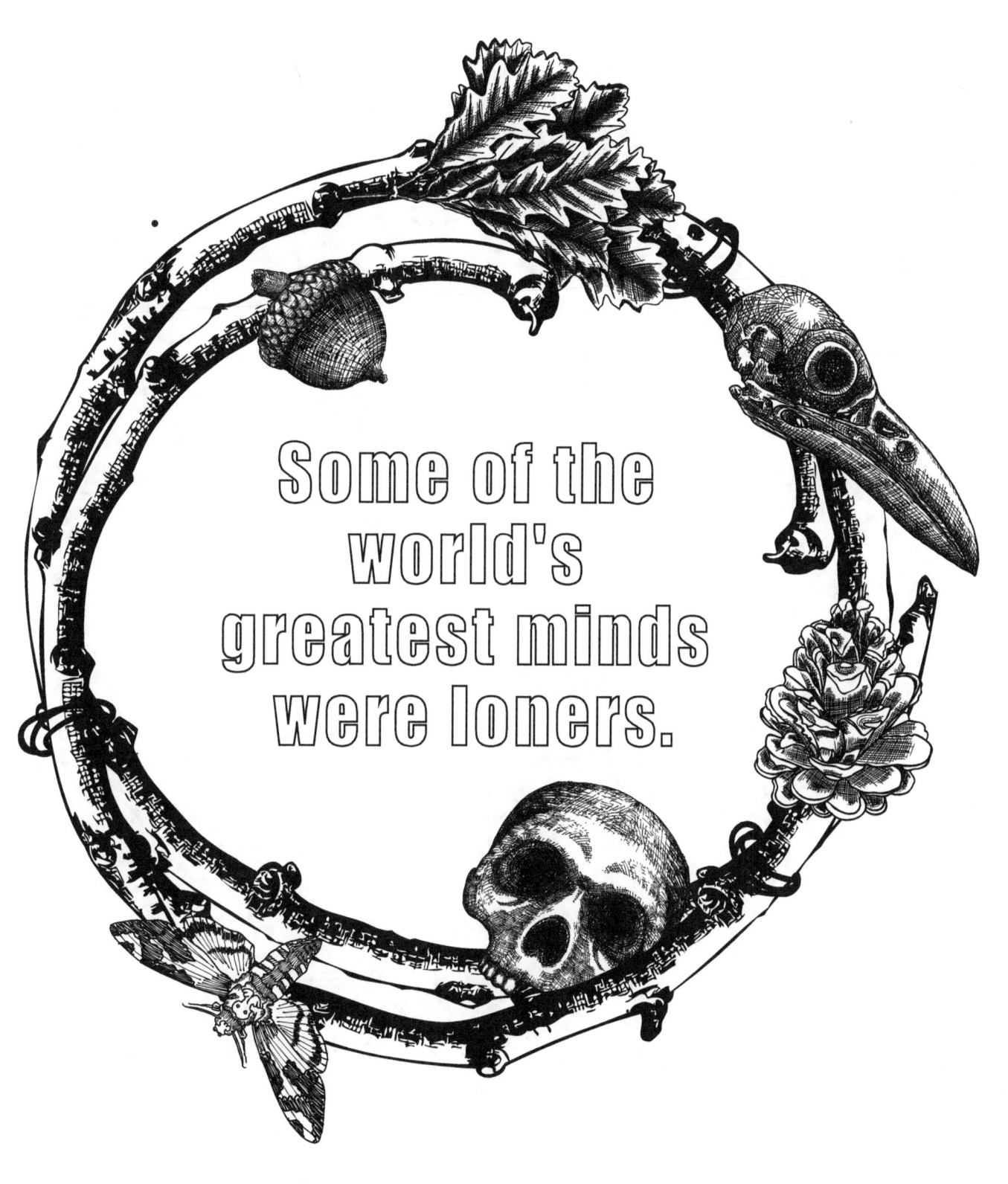

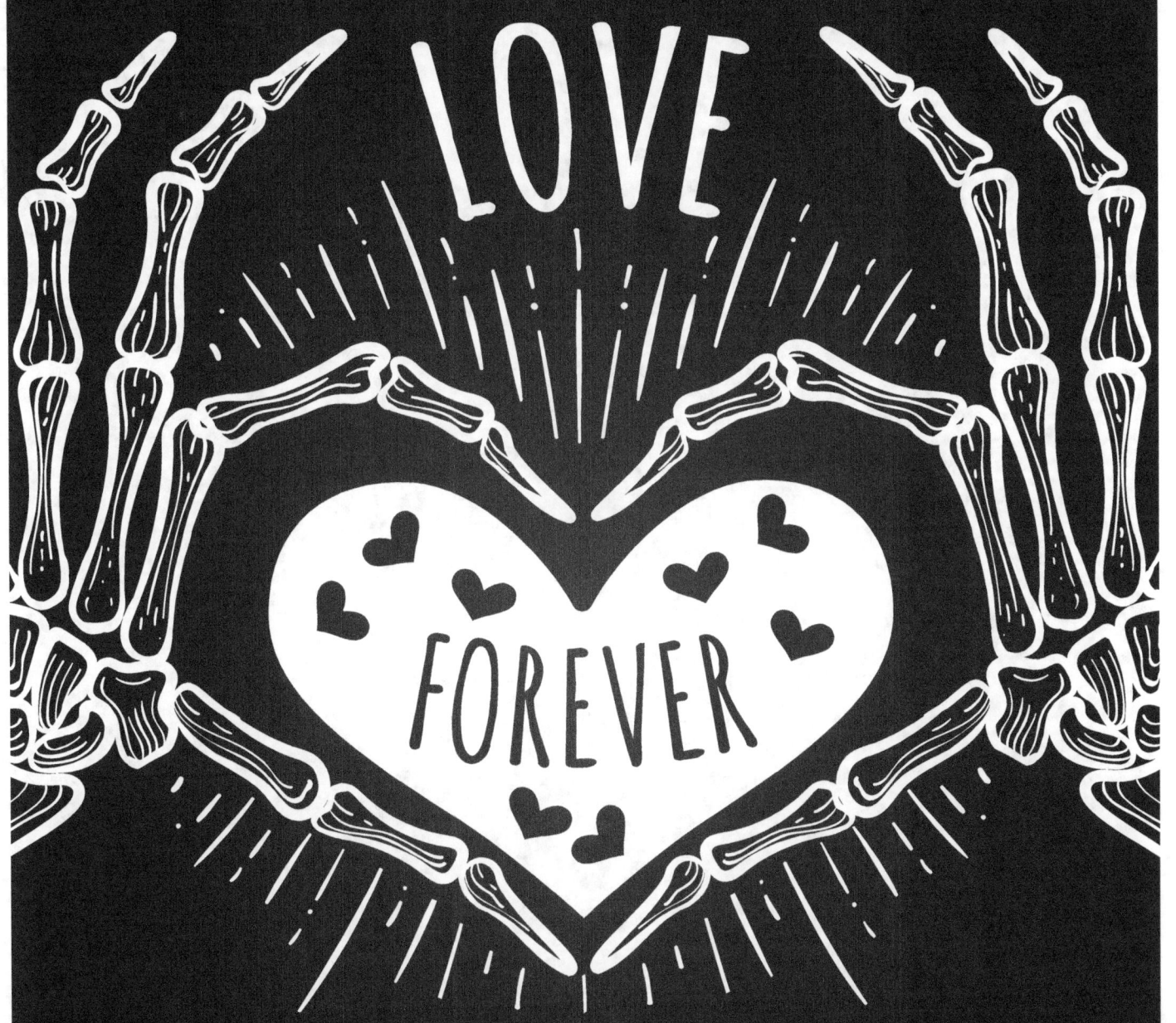